CSSE 11+ ESSEX TEST:
MATHS

In-depth Revision & Sample Practice Questions for the 11+ Maths Essex Grammar School Test

www.How2Become.com

As part of this product you have also received FREE access to online tests that will help you to pass your eleven plus (11+) assessments.

To gain access, simply go to:

www.MyEducationalTests.co.uk

Get more products for passing any test at:

www.How2Become.com

Orders: Please contact How2Become Ltd, Suite 3, 40 Churchill Square Business Centre, Kings Hill, Kent ME19 4YU.

You can order through Amazon.co.uk under ISBN 9781911259947, via the website www.How2Become.com, Gardners or Bertrams.

ISBN: 9781911259947

First published in 2017 by How2Become Ltd.

Copyright © 2017 How2Become.

All rights reserved. Apart from any permitted use under UK copyright law, no part of this publication may be reproduced or transmitted in any form or by any means, electronic or mechanical, including photocopying, recording, or any information, storage or retrieval system, without permission in writing from the publisher or under licence from the Copyright Licensing Agency Limited. Further details of such licenses (for reprographic reproduction) may be obtained from the Copyright Licensing Agency Ltd, Saffron House, 6-10 Kirby Street, London EC1N 8TS.

Typeset for How2Become Ltd by Gemma Butler.

Disclaimer

Every effort has been made to ensure that the information contained within this guide is accurate at the time of publication. How2Become Ltd is not responsible for anyone failing any part of any selection process as a result of the information contained within this guide. How2Become Ltd and their authors cannot accept any responsibility for any errors or omissions within this guide, however caused. No responsibility for loss or damage occasioned by any person acting, or refraining from action, as a result of the material in this publication can be accepted by How2Become Ltd.

The information within this guide does not represent the views of any third party service or organisation.

Contents

An Introduction to the Guide 6

Revision Tips for Parents 9

Useful Hints and Tips 13

The Structure of the Test 15

Practice Test Questions 1 17

Answers to Practice Test Questions 1 35

Practice Test Questions 2 43

Answers to Practice Test Questions 2 59

Practice Test Questions 3 65

Answers to Practice Test Questions 3 79

Final Advice 85

An Introduction to the Guide

The consortium of selective schools in Essex requires you to take **two** tests (one English, one Maths) in order to gain entry into any of the following ten schools:

1. Colchester County High School for Girls.
2. Colchester Royal Grammar School.
3. King Edward VI Grammar School.
4. Shoeburyness High School.
5. Southend High School for Boys.
6. Southend High School for Girls.
7. St. Bernard's High School for Girls.
8. St. Thomas More High School for Boys.
9. Westcliff High School for Boys.
10. Westcliff High School for Girls.

In this book we will be focusing on the Maths part of the exam. This book is designed to help you practise the skills you will need in order to pass and will provide you with an assortment of example questions similar to those you will face in the real exam.

We will also provide you with some useful hints and tips in order to best prepare yourself for the assessment.

Within this book you can expect to see the following types of Maths questions, and more:

Adding	Subtracting	Dividing	Multiplying
Fractions	Percentages	Decimals	Statistics
Charts	Mean, Mode, Median, Range	Areas and Perimeters	Number Sequences
Time	Conversions	Measurements	Money
Formulae	Data Interpretation	Shapes	Graphs

There is also another book in this series based on the type of questions you will have to answer on the English paper.

*Please note that the questions within this book are designed to give an idea of the types of questions that will be asked on the CSSE 11+ exam. These example questions will not correlate exactly to the questions that children will be required to answer on the real paper.

CHAPTER 1: REVISION TIPS FOR PARENTS

Revision Tips for Parents

- You may believe that the onus is really on your child's school to prepare them for their upcoming exam. While this is the case to some extent, it has been shown that parents' support and encouragement for their child to do even a small amount of practice outside of school can really improve their performance.

- Do not overload your child with stacks of work and make them feel overwhelmed. This will only serve to discourage them. As with many things, it is best to aim to break up their revision sessions into small, manageable chunks. This will ensure that their concentration levels remain high and they are able to take in the information that is being covered.

- Following on from the last point, make sure you schedule in plenty of rest breaks for your child. Allow them to go outside or participate in an activity that they enjoy doing. This boosts their energy and prepares them for the next time they sit down to study.

- Reward their progress and achievements. This doesn't have to mean anything extravagant, but when they have done well, or mastered a certain type of question that they had been struggling with, a small reward will make it all feel worthwhile.

- Have key notes or definitions placed around your home or your child's bedroom so that they are there to glance at every now and then. This will refresh the memory subliminally and help small portions of information to sink in. Visual aids are a great way to stimulate a child's brain.

- Encourage your child not to feel embarrassed about speaking up regarding topics they don't understand, so that they are able to talk through them.

- Plan to focus on a specific topic in each 'session'. This will ensure that it is not too overwhelming and your child's focus is set. Begin with a topic that they find the most challenging and interchange this with a topic that they are confident on – this will keep their confidence at a stable level.

- Encourage note taking and bullet-point making. If your child is simply reading through questions and working them out in their head, or speaking aloud the answers, it is less likely that the information will

REVISION TIPS FOR PARENTS

be retained than if it is written down.

- Make sure your child has an environment to study in which is as distraction free as possible. Somewhere not too noisy or cluttered will be the most productive kind of environment for them to work in. This will also mean that they will get more done as they avoid potential interruptions.

- Similarly, when your child has set aside some time to revise, make sure that the television is off, there are no phones available, and the focus is purely on the subject for that period of time. This means that once it is time for a break, these things will serve as a kind of reward for them in their free time.

- Once your child has become confident with a certain type of question, try encouraging them to practise under timed conditions. They do not necessarily have to do a whole past paper in one sitting, but even just a section whilst being timed will help to give them an idea of what it will feel like on the day of the exam.

- Gradually build up to longer sessions. If your child is having trouble concentrating, start with short twenty minute sessions and aim to build them up, over the course of their exam preparation, in small steps. This makes a lot more sense than sitting your child down for an hour or two and expecting them to stay concentrated from the outset.

- It may sound obvious, but make sure your child is getting enough sleep. If you haven't already, try and establish a solid routine. This will mean that they are able to concentrate and retain more information.

- It is especially important to try and ensure that your child gets adequate sleep the night before the exam. Try not to make them feel too stressed or pressured in the evening, and reassure them that you are confident in their abilities. This will alleviate some of the worrying that can occur in the days leading up to the exam.

- Let your child know that you are proud of them - whatever the outcome. They do not need the added pressure of worrying about potential failure. The best thing you can do is to encourage them, not to end up discouraging them by putting too much pressure on.

- Getting the right nutrition is also essential for everything from concentration, to sleep, to mood. Ensure your child is eating healthily and has a well-balanced diet. Consuming too much sugar or high-fat foods will make your child's energy levels peak and then crash and thus negatively affect their performance.

- Similarly, make sure your child is getting plenty of fresh air and exercise. They should be spending a small amount of time outside each day. This will also keep their concentration levels high and help them to get a refreshing sleep every night.

- Try not to leave revision to the last minute. This will only make your child feel unnecessarily stressed and anxious. If you start introducing small, manageable bites of revision a good amount of time before the exam, it will make for a much more productive outcome in the long run.

In summary, we recommend positively encouraging your child, helping them to revise gradually and progressively over time. Also, it's extremely important that you constantly aim to increase their confidence. Make sure they are getting everything they need at home such as a comfortable environment to study in and a well-balanced diet, and reward them for their achievements. We wish you and your child the best of luck in their exams!

CHAPTER 2:
USEFUL HINTS AND TIPS

Useful Hints and Tips

- The exam is designed specifically to test the kind of things you will have been learning in your Maths lessons at Key Stage 2. Therefore, it is important to brush up on all the key skills you have been working on at school, as well as trying your hand at some example practice questions such as those covered in this book.

- Ensure you understand what each question is asking you before you start to answer it. Re-read a question if you are unsure.

- Make sure you allocate your time in the exam wisely. Whilst it is important to make sure you understand and spend enough time on each question to get the best marks, you don't want to end up rushing any questions at the end of the paper.

- When you are given your test paper it will have recommended amounts of time to spend on each section of the exam. Whilst these times are only given as a guide, bear in mind that they have been formulated to try and help you make the most of your time, so try to stick to them wherever possible.

- The amount of marks that can be awarded for each question will be given in the margins of the test paper. This should also be an indicator for how long you should be spending on each question. Generally speaking, the higher the amount of marks you are able to get, the longer you should be spending answering the question.

- If you get really stuck on a question, don't spend too long thinking about it. Instead, move on to answering the rest of the paper to the best of your abilities, and leave some time at the end to come back and re-visit any questions you were unsure about the first time around.

- Make sure you practise all of the different types of questions before the exam. If there are certain types of questions you find harder to answer, or topics you struggle with, spend a little more time practising them than the ones you find easier.

- Try answering some of the example questions in this book under timed conditions. This will prepare you for what the exam will feel like on the day.

CHAPTER 3: THE STRUCTURE OF THE TEST

The Structure of the Test

The maths test is comprised of **one** test and **one** answer booklet is provided.

There are a total of **sixty marks** available for the exam, and you are given **sixty minutes** to complete the test.

It is recommended that you answer all the questions you can in good time, and not spend too long on a question you are not sure on. This means that you can leave yourself time at the end of the test to go over and try again on any questions you were unsure of the first time around.

You will **not** be able to use a calculator during the test and you will be provided with space on the answer booklet to show your workings if necessary.

The test will include an array of different types of maths problems you will have studied at school.

The exam board advise that once the test has commenced, you will be unable to ask about any of the questions within it.

The number of available marks for each question will be given in the margin of each page.

CHAPTER 4: PRACTICE TEST QUESTIONS 1

18   CSSE ESSEX 11+ TEST: MATHS

Practice Test Questions 1

60 marks available in total

Question 1

    a) Calculate: **16.09 + 5.43**

Answer
> 11·06

    b) Add: **565 + 9126**

Answer
> 9,691

(2 marks)

Question 2

    a) Work out the difference between: **8,365 and 645**

Answer
> 7,720

    b) Calculate: **47.06 – 36.08**

Answer
> 10.08

(2 marks)

Question 3

    a) Multiply: **41 x 230**

Answer
> 9,430

b) Calculate: **12 x 3.9**

Answer: 46.8

(2 marks)

Question 4

a) Divide: **144 ÷ 9**

Answer: 16

b) Calculate: **18 ÷ 0.3**

Answer: 0.6

(2 marks)

Question 5

The following calculations have **one** digit missing. Where there is a question mark, find the digit that completes the calculation.

a) 72 + 1?7 = 259

Answer: 8

b) 0.4? − 0.13 = 0.29

Answer: 2

c) 21 x 9?8 = 20,748

Answer: 8

20   CSSE ESSEX 11+ TEST: MATHS

d) $621 - 513 = 10?$

Answer   8

e) $5.5 \div 0.? = 11$

Answer   5

f) $2? - 29 = -6$

Answer   3

(6 marks)

Question 6

Assume that the letters of the alphabet have the following ascending values:

$A = 1$, $B = 2$, $C = 3$, $D = 4$ and so on, and answer the following questions by adding up the values of the letters.

For example, the word **DARK** $= 4 + 1 + 18 + 11 =$ a value of **34**

a) What is the value of the word **LIST**?

Answer   60

b) Using the same letter value system, sort the following words in ascending order according to value (lowest to highest).

VOTE   PINS   WORD

PRACTICE TEST QUESTIONS 1

> **Lowest**
>
> ....*Pins*........
>
> ....*Word*........
>
> ....*Vote*........
>
> **Highest**

c) Find a three letter word in the English language that can be added to the word **'FAR'** to make the total value of the word **'CROWD'**.

FAR + ... = CROWD

In these next questions, the letters of the alphabet have the same number values (A = 1, B = 2, C = 3, D = 4 and so on), however this time you must *multiply* the numbers to reach your answers.

For example, the word **FEED** = 6 x 5 x 5 x 4 = a value of **600**

d) What is the value of the word **JADE**?

Answer

CSSE ESSEX 11+ TEST: MATHS

e) Using the same letter value system, and by multiplying the values, sort the following words in ascending order according to value (lowest to highest).

RAG   **KID**   **LED**

Lowest

....

....

....

Highest

(5 marks)

Question 7

Take a look at the following sweet shop price list:

WHITE CHOCOLATE MICE.................£O.2O EACH

BANANA SWEETS.....................£O.I3 EACH

STRAWBERRY LACES..................£O.25 EACH

LIQUORICE PIECES....................£O.I6 EACH

a) Harry filled up a bag with sweets for him and his friend. In total he had 6 white mice, 7 banana sweets, 3 strawberry laces, and 5 liquorice pieces. He paid using a five pound note. How much change did he get back?

Answer

b) Martha chose a bag to share between her and her family. In total she had 12 strawberry laces, 15 white mice, 25 banana sweets and 8 liquorice pieces. What was the total cost?

Answer

(2 marks)

Question 8

See below a table of values representing the formula 5 $(y + 2)$. Some of the boxes have already been filled in. Using the values already in the table, fill in the missing gaps.

y	5 $(y+2)$
5	35
12	
	50

(2 marks)

Question 9

Mark took his new drone out for a test. He measured how high it flew. The chart below shows the results.

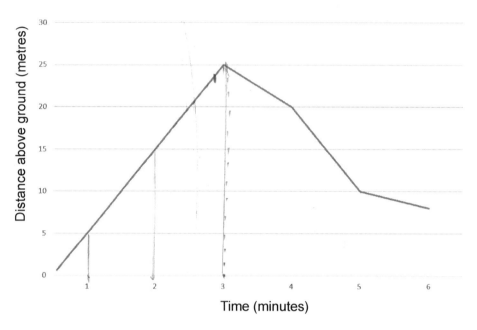

a) How long did he fly his drone for overall?

…………..minutes

b) How high did he manage to get the drone at 3 minutes?

…………..metres

c) What was the plane doing from 1 to 3 minutes? Circle your answer.

Climbing   Falling   Remaining at a steady height

(3 marks)

PRACTICE TEST QUESTIONS 1

Question 10

a) How many grams are in 4.5kg?

................g

b) A jug contains 0.72 litres. How much is this in *ml*?

................*ml*

(2 marks)

Question 11

Six children took a literacy test. Their scores were as follows:

67, 58, 54, 49, 65, 55.

a) What was the mean (average) score?

Answer

b) What is the range?

Answer

(2 marks)

Question 12

Look at the following number sequences and fill in the missing gaps:

a) 1, 2, 4, 7, 11, 16, ... 29, ...

26   CSSE ESSEX 11+ TEST: MATHS

b) 667, 638, …….…….., 586, 563, 542, …….…..…

c) 7, 17, 15, 27, …….……., 37, 31, …….………., 39

(3 marks)

Question 13

Fill in the gaps in these number sequences. The rules will be given above.

a) The rule here is "divide by 5".

10,000, 2,000, ……….., 80, ……….,

b) The rule here is "subtract 1/8".

……….., 1/4, 1/8, ………. -1/8, -1/4

c) The rule here is "multiply by 10, then add 5".

……….., 7.5, 80, ……….., 8,055, 80,555

d) The rule here is "divide by 4"

……….., 0.8, 0.2, ……….., 0.0125

(4 marks)

PRACTICE TEST QUESTIONS 1 27

Question 14

For the following questions, there is one digit wrong in each calculation. They can be corrected by changing **one digit** in each question to the number **5**. For the following questions, find out which digit should be replaced and re-write the calculation underneath so that it is correct.

a) 87 – 62 = 29

Answer

b) 663 + 92 = 745

Answer

c) 84 + (41 x 3) = 219

Answer

d) 946 + (19 x 13) = 1,203

Answer

(4 marks)

Question 15

A total of thirty adults were asked how many cars were owned by their household. The results were as follows:

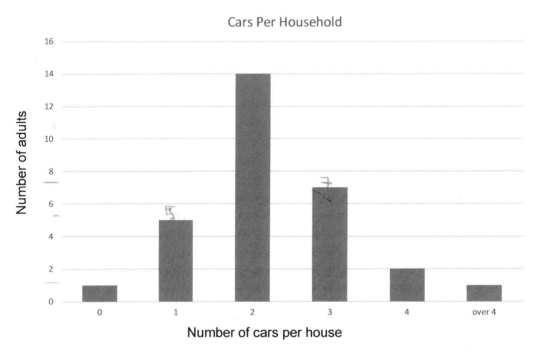

a) How many adults had **2 cars** in their household?

Answer

b) How many adults had **more than 2** cars in their household?

Answer

c) The adult that answered "over 4" had 6 cars. With this in mind, how many cars do **all** the adults have **combined**?

Answer

(3 marks)

Question 16

Amreen has a piece of ribbon which measures 5m and 45cm long. She cuts off a piece to wrap a present which measures 439cm. How long is the piece she now has remaining, in centimetres?

..........cm

(1 mark)

Question 17

A group of fifty people were asked about whether they owned cats, dogs, both, or none. The results are laid out in the Venn diagram below.

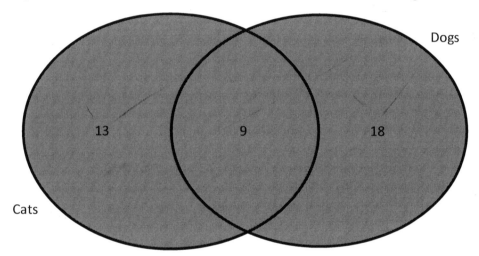

a) How many people who were surveyed had *only* dogs?

Answer

b) How many people had *no* cats *or* dogs?

Answer

c) How many people in the survey had cats?

Answer

(3 marks)

Question 18

Use the following five number cards to complete the calculations below:

| 5 | 9 | 3 | 7 | 8 |

In the first two questions, you will need to use all 5 number cards.

a)

 = 671

b)

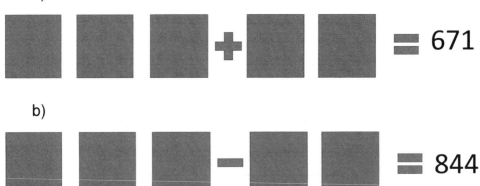 = 844

For this question, you will need to use 4 of the 5 number cards.

c)

 = 63

(3 marks)

Question 19

For the following formulas, give the value of x when $y = 6$.

a) $x = y - 8 + 1$

$x =$

b) $x = y^2 + 7$

$x =$

c) $x = 11 (y - 3)$

$x =$

(3 marks)

Question 20

Theo is arranging blocks into patterns. The blocks he is using are all the same size.

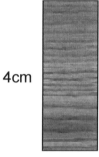

This is the first pattern he makes.

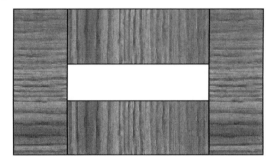

a) What is the area of the shape Theo would require to fill the gap in the middle?

Answer [ ]

b) What is the perimeter of the shape that Theo creates?

Answer [ ]

PRACTICE TEST QUESTIONS 1   33

c) Theo decides on a different pattern. What is the perimeter of this new pattern?

Answer [   ]

d) What is the total area of this new pattern?

Answer [   ]

(4 marks)

Question 21

a) Pep is shopping for clothes in the sale. He finds a jacket he likes. The original price was £75.00. There is a tag on the jacket saying it is now 25% off. How much is the jacket?

£.............

b) Pep's friend tells him that tomorrow the shop will put a 30% discount on the jacket. How much money will Pep save if he buys the jacket with a 30% discount, rather than a 25% discount?

£.............

(2 marks)

[END OF PRACTICE TEST ONE]

CHAPTER 5:
ANSWERS TO PRACTICE TEST QUESTIONS 1

36 CSSE ESSEX 11+ TEST: MATHS

Answers to Practice Test Questions 1

60 marks available in total

Q1.

a) 21.52

b) 9,691

(2 marks)

Q2.

a) 7,720

b) 10.98

(2 marks)

Q3.

a) 9,430

b) 46.8

(2 marks)

Q4.

a) 16

b) 60

(2 marks)

Q5.

a) 8

b) 2

c) 8

d) 8

ANSWERS TO PRACTICE TEST QUESTIONS 1

e) 5

f) 3

(6 marks)

Q6.

a) 12 + 9 + 19 + 20 = **60**

b) Pins: 16 + 9 + 14 + 19 = **58**

Word: 23 + 15 + 18 + 4 = **60**

Vote: 22 + 15 + 20 + 5 = **62**

c) Crowd = 3 + 18 + 15 + 23 + 4 = **63**,

Far = 6 + 1 + 18 = **25**,

So the missing word must come to a total of **38**

For example, "Mud" = 13 + 21 + 4 = **38**

Any three letter word that comes to a total of 38 is acceptable.

d) 10 x 1 x 4 x 5 = **200**

e) Rag: 18 x 1 x 7 = **126**

Led: 12 x 5 x 4 = **240**

Kid: 11 x 9 x 4 = **396**

(5 marks)

Q7.

a) **£1.34**

(£1.20 + 0.91 + 0.75 + 0.80 = £3.66

£5.00 – 3.66 = 1.34)

b) **£10.53**

(£3.00 + £3.00 + £3.25 + £1.28 = 10.53)

(2 marks)

Q8.

Box 1: **70** (12 + 12 = 14, 14 x 5 = 70)

Box 2: **8** (8 + 2 = 10, 10 x 5 = 50)

(2 marks)

Q9.

a) 6 minutes

b) 25 metres

c) Climbing

(3 marks)

Q10.

a) 4500 g.

b) 720ml.

(2 marks)

Q11.

a) **58** (67 + 60 + 54 + 49 + 65 + 55 = 350)

350 divided by 6 = 58.3 re-occurring so 58

b) **18** (67 - 49 = 18)

(2 marks)

Q12.

a) 22, 37 (pattern is add 1, add 2, add 3 and so on).

b) 611, 523 (pattern is minus 29, minus 27, minus 25 and so on).

c) 23, 47 (pattern is add 10 minus 2, add 12 minus 4, add 14 minus

ANSWERS TO PRACTICE TEST QUESTIONS 1   39

6 and so on).

(3 marks)

Q13.

a) 400, 16

b) 3/8, 0

c) 0.25, 805

d) 3.2, 0.05

(4 marks)

Q14.

a) $87 - 62 = 25$

b) $653 + 92 = 745$

c) $84 + (45 \times 3) = 219$

d) $956 + (19 \times 13) = 1{,}203$

(4 marks)

Q15.

a) **14**

b) **10** (7 + 2 + 1)

c) **68** (5 x 1 = 5) + (14 x 2 = 28) + (7 x 3 = 21) + (2 x 4 = 8) + (1 x 6 = 6)

(3 marks)

Q16.

106 centimetres

(1 mark)

40   CSSE ESSEX 11+ TEST: MATHS

Q17.

    a) **18**

    b) **10** (18 + 13 + 9) = 40

    50 − 40 = 10

    c) **22** (13 + 9)

(3 marks)

Q18.

    a) **598** + **73** = 671 *alternate answer is 593 + 78 = 671

    b) **897** − **53** = 844 *alternate answer is 879 + 35 = 844

    c) **98** − (**7** x **5**) = 63

(3 marks)

Q19.

    a) x = **-1**

    b) x = **43**

    c) x = **33**

(3 marks)

Q20.

    a) 4cm²

    b) 22cm

    c) 20cm

    d) 24cm²

(4 marks)

Q21.

a) **£56.25** (75 ÷ 100 = 0.75 x 25 = 18.75

75 − 18.75 = 56.25)

c) **£3.75** (75 ÷ 100 = 0.75 x 30 = 22.50

22.50 − 18.75 = 3.75)

(2 marks)

CHAPTER 6: PRACTICE TEST QUESTIONS 2

CSSE ESSEX 11+ TEST: MATHS

Practice Test Questions 2

60 marks available in total

Question 1

a) Calculate: **19.01 + 17.43**

Answer

b) Add: **4,982 + 297**

Answer

(2 marks)

Question 2

a) Work out the difference between: **6,382 – 409**

Answer

b) Calculate: **74.28 – 39.47**

Answer

(2 marks)

Question 3

a) Multiply: **64 x 520**

Answer

PRACTICE TEST QUESTIONS 2   45

b) Calculate: **25 x 9.7**

Answer

(2 marks)

Question 4

a) Divide: **372 ÷ 6**

Answer

b) Calculate: **20 ÷ 0.8**

Answer

(2 marks)

Question 5

a) Work out the value of: (8 + 7) x (5 + 3)

Answer

b) Calculate the value of: 9 + (5 x 5) + 18

Answer

c) Work out the value of: (9 – 2) x 9 + 2

Answer

46 CSSE ESSEX 11+ TEST: MATHS

d) Calculate the value of: 7 x (4 + 3) + 8

Answer

(4 marks)

Question 6

For the following formulas, calculate the value of x when $y = 7$.

a) $x = y - 6 + 3$

$x =$

b) $x = y^2 - 13$

$x =$

c) $x = 21 (y + 4)$

$x =$

(3 marks)

Question 7

Kudzi sells cupcake making kits. These are her prices:

Cupcake kit: £5.50 each

Decorations priced at 25p each

a) Sandra purchased 2 kits with some decorations. She paid £15.25 in total. How many decorations did she buy?

Answer [ ]

Kudzi's suppliers' prices go up causing her to have to increase her prices by 20%.

b) How much does a kit cost now (without decorations)?

Answer [ ]

c) Sandra wants to buy some decorations to use with her existing kits. She plans to make a number of cupcakes to sell at a local charity fundraiser. Given Kudzi's new prices, how much will Sandra pay for 150 decorations?

Answer [ ]

d) Ali wants to buy a kit and some decorations. He has £7.50 to spend. With Kudzi's new prices, how many decorations could Ali afford?

Answer [ ]

(4 marks)

Question 8

a) A bag of sugar has 1,262g remaining in it. How much is this in kg?

............kg

b) A sunflower grows to a total of 1,023mm tall. How tall is this in cm?

............cm

c) Calculate the total value of the following, and provide your answer in *cm*:

2cm + 1.5mm + 0.6m.

............cm

d) A carton has 0.45 litres remaining in it. How much is this in *ml*?

............ml

e) The area of a tile is 5cm x 5cm = 25cm². What is this area written in mm²?

............mm²

(5 marks)

Question 9

Fred is using a number machine to perform certain calculations.

His number machine looks like this:

INPUT ➡ (x5) ➡ (+9) ➡ OUTPUT

a) What output will Fred find if the number 62 is the input?

Answer

b) Fred finds an output of the number 84. What number did he input into the machine?

Answer

Fred tries another number machine. This time the calculations are hidden and need to be calculated.

The other machine looks like this:

INPUT ➡ (x?) ➡ (-?) ➡ OUTPUT

c) Fred input into the machine 12 and the output was 58. In the same machine, he input 24 and the output was 118. What calculations did the machine perform?

x...............   - ....

d) Using the same machine, calculate the output that Fred would achieve when the input is 6.

Answer

(4 marks)

50 CSSE ESSEX 11+ TEST: MATHS

Question 10

See below a table of values representing the formula 9 $(x + 5)$. Some of the boxes have already been filled in. Using the values already in the table, fill in the missing gaps.

x	9 $(x + 5)$
10	135
	81
6	

(2 marks)

Question 11

A group of children participated in a spelling test. Their scores were as follows:

30	20	18	25	20	22	27	20	24	24

a) What is the *mode*?

Answer

b) What is the *mean* score?

Answer

PRACTICE TEST QUESTIONS 2

c) 2 more children submit their scores later. They are: 29 and 17. Does this change the mean score?

Yes / No

d) Using all the scores, including the ones submitted later, calculate the *range*.

Answer

(4 marks)

Question 12 ●

a) Calculate: 12^2

Answer

b) How many *square numbers* exist between the values of 8 to 50?

Answer

c) Work out the value of 14 x 14.

Answer

d) How else could 14 x 14 be expressed?

Answer

(4 marks)

Question 13

Abe has some spare pieces of wood in his shed. He is trying to work out if he can make a box with them. Below is a chart showing some of their sizes.

Area (cm²)	Perimeter (cm)	Length (cm)	Width (cm)
36		12	
		6	5
64			8

Fill in the blanks to make the chart complete.

(6 marks)

Question 14

The following images are of unfolded dice. For each question, indicate how many dots will be on the *opposite* side to the **four** dots when the dice are folded.

a)

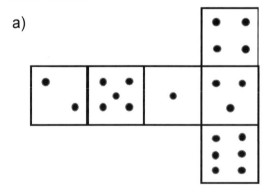

Answer

PRACTICE TEST QUESTIONS 2 53

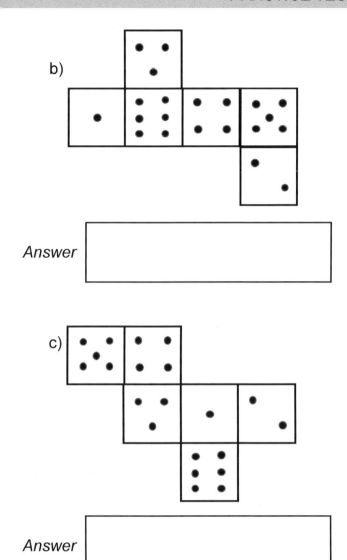

Answer

Answer

d)

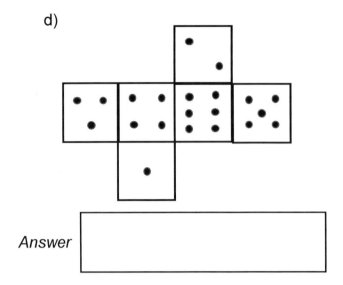

Answer [   ]

(4 marks)

Question 15

Fill in the missing gaps for the following fraction calculations.

a) $\dfrac{6}{10} + \dfrac{\Box}{5} = 1$

b) $\dfrac{1}{4} + \dfrac{3}{5} = \dfrac{17}{\Box}$

c) $\dfrac{5}{16} - \dfrac{1}{\Box} = \dfrac{1}{16}$

d) $\dfrac{2}{\Box} + \dfrac{1}{10} = \dfrac{1}{2}$

(4 marks)

Question 16

The following sign shows the opening times for a zoo.

Zoo Opening Times

March - June	Daily	9:00am to 5:30pm
July - August	Daily	9:00am to 8:00pm
September - February	Saturday and Sunday	10:00am to 4:00pm

Last admission is 2 hours before the zoo closes.

a) How many months of the year does the zoo close on weekdays?

................months

b) Kelly goes to the zoo in July. She arrives at 2pm. How many hours can she spend there until it closes?

................hours

c) Marcus has a season ticket for 2017, allowing him multiple visits at a reduced price. He visits the zoo the following times throughout the year:

- Once in January, arriving when the park opens and leaving 2 hours before last admission.

- Once in May, arriving at 3:00pm and leaving an hour before closing time.

- Once in July, arriving at one hour after the park opens and leaving 5 hours before closing time.

- Once in August, arriving at 4pm and staying until closing time.

How much time did Marcus spend in the zoo in 2017 in hours and minutes?

…………….hours……………..minutes

d) Misha and her friends want to visit the zoo in June. What is the *latest* time they will be able to enter?

Answer

(4 marks)

Question 17

For the following questions, work out the value of the missing angle.

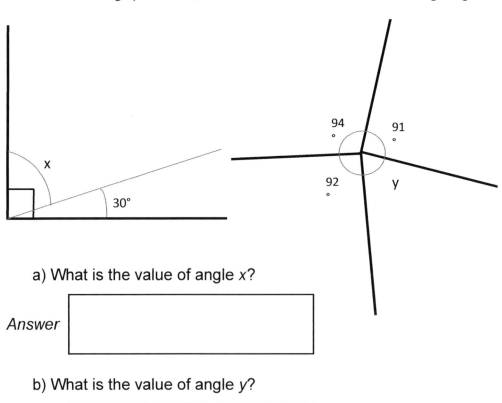

a) What is the value of angle x?

Answer

b) What is the value of angle y?

Answer

(2 marks)

Question 18

a) $x + x + x = 9$

$x + x + y = 16$

$y + x + z = 22$

What is the value of z?

$z =$

b) $p + p + q = 18$

$q + q + q = 30$

$p + s + q = 28$

What is the value of s?

$s =$

(2 marks)

[END OF PRACTICE TEST TWO]

CHAPTER 7: ANSWERS TO PRACTICE TEST QUESTIONS 2

60 CSSE ESSEX 11+ TEST: MATHS

Answers to Practice Test Questions 2

60 marks _available in total_

Q1.

    a) 36.44

    b) 5,279

(2 marks)

Q2.

    a) 5,973

    b) 34.81

(2 marks)

Q3.

    a) 33,280

    b) 242.5

(2 marks)

Q4.

    a) 62

    b) 25

(2 marks)

Q5.

    a) $15 \times 8 = \mathbf{120}$

    b) $9 + 25 + 18 = \mathbf{52}$

ANSWERS TO PRACTICE TEST QUESTIONS 2

c) 7 x 9 + 2 = **65**

d) 7 x 7 ׀ 8 = **57**

(4 marks)

Q6.

a) $x = 4$

b) $x = 36$

c) $x = 231$

(3 marks)

Q7.

a) 17

b) **£6.60** (5.5 ÷ 100 x 20 = 1.1

5.5 + 1.1 = £6.60)

c) **£45.00** (0.25 ÷ 100 x 20 = 0.30

0.30 x 150 = £45.00)

d) **3 decorations** (7.50 – 6.60 = 0.90

0.90 ÷ 30 = 3)

(4 marks)

Q8.

a) 1.262kg

b) 102.3cm

c) **62.15cm** (2 + 0.15 + 60 = 62.15)

d) 450ml

e) 2500mm²

(5 marks)

62 CSSE ESSEX 11+ TEST: MATHS

Q9.

a) **319** (62 x 5 + 9 = 319)

b) **15** (84 − 9 ÷ 5 = 15)

c) **x 5 − 2** (12 x 5 -2 = 58) (24 x 5 -2 = 118)

d) **28** (6 x 5 − 2 = 28)

(4 marks)

Q10.

Box 1: **4** (4 + 5 x 9 = 81)

Box 2: **99** (6 + 5 x 9 = 99)

(2 marks)

Q11.

a) **20** (most frequently occurring number)

b) **23** (30 + 20 + 18 + 25 + 20 + 22 + 27 + 20 + 24 + 24 = 230) ÷ 10 = 23

c) **No** (30 + 20 + 18 + 25 + 20 + 22 + 27 + 20 + 24 + 24 + 29 + 17 = 276) ÷ 12 = 23

d) **13** (30 − 17 = 13)

(4 marks)

Q12.

a) 144

b) **5** (9, 16, 25, 36, 49)

c) 196

d) 14^2

(4 marks)

ANSWERS TO PRACTICE TEST QUESTIONS 2

Q13.

Area (cm²)	Perimeter (cm)	Length (cm)	Width (cm)
36	30	12	3
30	22	6	5
64	32	8	8

(6 marks)

Q14.

a) 6

b) 1

c) 6

d) 5

(4 marks)

Q15.

a) 2

b) 20

c) 4

d) 5

(4 marks)

Q16.

a) **6 months** (September, October, November, December, January, February).

b) **6 hours** (2pm until 8pm).

c) **12 hours and 30 minutes** (10am to 12 noon = **2 hours** + 3pm to 4:30pm = **1 hour 30 minutes** + 10am to 3pm = **5 hours** + 4pm to 8pm = **4 hours**).

d) **3:30pm** (Last admissions are 2 hours before closing time which is 5:30pm in June).

(4 marks)

Q17.

a) 60°

b) 83°

(2 marks)

Q18.

a) **9** ($x = 3$, $y = 10$, $z = 9$)

b) **14** ($p = 4$, $q = 10$, $s = 14$)

(2 marks)

CHAPTER 8: PRACTICE TEST QUESTIONS 3

66 CSSE ESSEX 11+ TEST: MATHS

Practice Test Questions 3

60 marks available in total

Question 1

a) Calculate: **22.98 + 5.79**

Answer

b) Add: **674 + 2,098**

Answer

(2 marks)

Question 2

a) Work out: **3,567 - 908**

Answer

b) Calculate: **38.63 − 22.13**

Answer

(2 marks)

Question 3

a) Multiply: **20 x 690**

Answer

PRACTICE TEST QUESTIONS 3

b) Calculate: **32 x 8.5**

Answer

(2 marks)

Question 4

a) Divide: **224 ÷ 14**

Answer

b) Calculate: **90 ÷ 0.2**

Answer

(2 marks)

Question 5

The following calculations have **one** digit missing. Where there is a question mark, find the digit that completes the calculation.

a) 567 + 3?6 = 873

Answer

b) 0.9? – 0.55 = 0.41

Answer

68   CSSE ESSEX 11+ TEST: MATHS

c) 66 x 2**?**4 = 15,444

Answer

d) 633 − 481 = 15**?**

Answer

e) 10.6 ÷ 0.**?** = 53

Answer

f) 3**?** − 74 = - 35

Answer

(6 marks)

Question 6

A survey was conducted on 30 students' favourite core subject. The pie chart below shows the results.

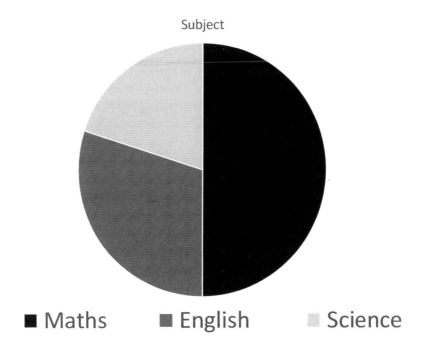

a) How many children chose Maths as their favourite subject?

Answer

b) 30% of children chose English as their favourite subject. How many children is this?

Answer

c) What percentage of children chose Science as their favourite subject?

Answer

(3 marks)

70 CSSE ESSEX 11+ TEST: MATHS

Question 7

Have a look over the bus timetable below.

Green Street	07:32	08:40	09:55
Lower Road	07:46	08:54	10:09
Acer Lane	07:58	09:06	10:21
Central High Street	08:24	09:32	10:47
Bus Station Stop 4	08:36	09:44	10:59

a) Luke arrives at Acer Lane Bus Stop at 09:57. How long will he have to wait before his bus arrives?

...............*minutes*

b) Once on the bus, how many minutes will it take for Luke to get to Bus Station Stop 4?

...............*minutes*

c) On Monday, Anil gets the bus at 8:40 from Green Street to Acre Lane. On Tuesday he gets the 7:32 bus from Green Street and gets off at Bus Stop Station 4. How long in total did he spend on the bus over the two days?

...............*hours*...............*minutes*

d) Ifkhan misses his usual bus (the 07:32 from Green Street). How much later will he arrive at the Central High Street on the next bus than he usually would?

...............*hours*...............*minutes*

PRACTICE TEST QUESTIONS 3 71

e) Rita needs to get to a meeting that starts at 10:00. It takes her 12 minutes to walk there from the central high street. She catches the bus at 08:54 from Lower Road. How many minutes early will she arrive to the meeting?

.............*minutes*   *(5 marks)*

Question 8

a) What is the value of 12 x 17?

Answer

b) Calculate 9^3.

Answer

c) List the prime numbers between 10 and 30.

Answer

d) Calculate $5^2 + 4^3$.

Answer

e) List the square numbers between 3 and 30.

Answer

CSSE ESSEX 11+ TEST: MATHS

f) The sum of 2 square numbers is 365. One of the square numbers is 14^2 (196). What is the other square number?

Answer

(6 marks)

Question 9

a) What is a third of £96?

Answer

b) Calculate 25% of £96.

Answer

c) A pair of trousers are reduced in the sale by 20%. They originally cost £35. What is the new price?

Answer

d) A pair of shorts that originally cost £30 are reduced in the sale by £12.00. What percentage discount has been applied?

Answer

(4 marks)

Question 10

Christine is a florist. She is selling various bouquets of flowers and optional extras for Valentine's Day. This is her current price list.

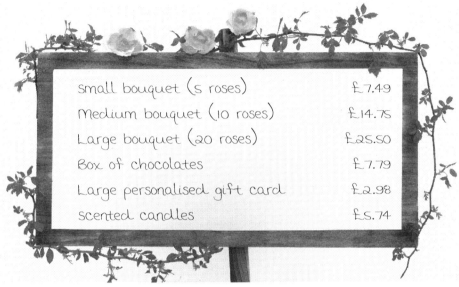

a) Helena wants to buy her partner a medium bouquet, a box of chocolates and a gift card. What will the total of her spend be?

Answer

b) How much change would Christine give to a customer who purchased a small bouquet, two sets of scented candles and a gift card with a twenty pound note and a five pound note?

Answer

c) One customer had fifty pounds to spend on flowers. They bought **three** bouquets and their change from a fifty pound note was £2.26. Which three bouquets did they purchase?

Answer

(3 marks)

Question 11

Femi is hosting a competition to raise money for charity. He sells raffle tickets at his school with values from 1 to 40. The winning ticket will receive a prize.

a) Millie buys 2 tickets. What is the probability of her winning the prize? Write your answer as a fraction *in its simplest form.*

Answer

b) Millie's friend Poppy says to her that she is *twice* as likely to have a ticket with a prime number as one with a factor of 12. Is Poppy correct?

Answer

c) Poppy also says to Millie that she is more likely to have a ticket with a prime number than one which is a multiple of 3. Is Poppy correct this time?

Answer

(3 marks)

Question 12

Below is a 'magic square'. In a magic square, all rows, columns and diagonals must add up to the same number. For the question below, work out the missing numbers.

a)

3		15
19	7	
-1	11	11

b)

12		2
0	10	20
18	4	

(4 marks)

Question 13

Fill in the missing gaps in the chart showing the area, perimeter, length and width of shapes.

Area (cm²)	Perimeter (cm)	Length (cm)	Width (cm)
121		11	
		8	7
105			5

(6 marks)

Question 14

The cube below measures 16cm x 16cm x 16cm.

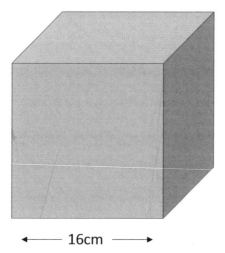

16cm

a) How many edges are there on a cube?

Answer

PRACTICE TEST QUESTIONS 3

b) "A cube has half the number of faces as it does edges". True or false?

Answer

c) Half of the faces of the cube are painted. What area is painted?

……….cm²   (3 marks)

Question 15

The charts below are completed by multiplying the two numbers directly below them. Take a look at the example below:

		350		
	10		35	
2		5		7

Now fill in the missing three gaps in the charts below to complete them:

a)

	42			
		7		4

b)

	27			
		3		3

(6 marks)

78   CSSE ESSEX 11+ TEST: MATHS

Question 16

For the following statements, indicate whether they are true or false with a tick ✓ for true and a cross ✗ for false.

a)	Quadrilaterals are shapes which are always flat.	
b)	The interior angles of a quadrilateral add up to 360°.	
c)	The two diagonals of a rectangle are never equal in length.	

(3 marks)

[END OF PRACTICE TEST THREE]

CHAPTER 9: ANSWERS TO PRACTICE TEST QUESTIONS 3

80 CSSE ESSEX 11+ TEST: MATHS

Answers to Practice Test Questions 3

60 marks available in total

Q1.

    a) 28.77

    b) 2,772

              (2 marks)

Q2.

    a) 2,659

    b) 16.5

              (2 marks)

Q3.

    a) 13,800

    b) 272

              (2 marks)

Q4.

    a) 16

    b) 450

              (2 marks)

Q5.

    a) 0

    b) 6

    c) 3

ANSWERS TO PRACTICE TEST QUESTIONS 3

d) 2

e) 2

f) 9

(6 marks)

Q6.

a) 15

b) 9

c) 20%

(3 marks)

Q7.

a) 24 minutes

b) 38 minutes

c) 1 hours 30 minutes

d) 1 hour 8 minutes

e) 16 minutes

(5 marks)

Q8.

a) 204

b) 729

c) 11, 13, 17, 19, 23, 29

d) **89** (25 + 64)

e) 4, 9, 16, 25

f) 13^2 = 169 (+14^2 = 196 = 365)

(6 marks)

82 CSSE ESSEX 11+ TEST: MATHS

Q9.

a) £32

b) £24

c) £28

d) 40%

(4 marks)

Q10.

a) **£25.52** (14.75 + 7.79 + 2.98)

b) **£3.05** (7.49 + 5.74 + 5.74 + 2.98 = 21.95, 25 – 21.95 = 3.05)

c) **One large bouquet, one medium bouquet, one small bouquet.** (25.50 + 14.75 + 7.49 = 47.74, 50 – 47.74 = 2.26)

(3 marks)

Q11.

a) **1/20** (2/40)

b) **Yes**

Factors of 12: 1,2,3,3,6,12. (**6**)

Prime numbers between 1 and 40: 2, 3, 5, 7, 11, 13, 17, 19, 23, 29, 31, 37. (**12**)

c) **No**

Multiples of 3 from 1 to 40: 3, 6, 9, 12, 15, 18, 21, 24, 27, 30, 33, 36, 39 (**13**)

Prime numbers between 1 and 40: 2, 3, 5, 7, 11, 13, 17, 19, 23, 29, 31, 37. (**12**)

(3 marks)

ANSWERS TO PRACTICE TEST QUESTIONS 3

Q12.

a) **3, -5** (all rows, columns and diagonals add up to **21**)

b) **16, 8** (all rows, columns and diagonals add up to **30**)

(4 marks)

Q13.

Area (cm²)	Perimeter (cm)	Length (cm)	Width (cm)
121	44	11	11
56	30	8	7
105	52	21	5

(6 marks)

Q14.

a) 12

b) **True** (it has 6 faces)

c) 768cm²

(3 marks)

Q15.

a)

		1,176		
	42		28	
6		7		4

b)

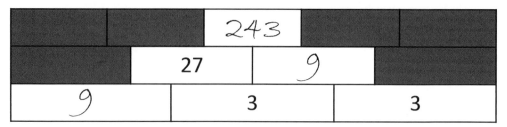

(6 marks)

Q16.

a) ✓ True

b) ✓ True

c) ✗ False

(3 marks)

CHAPTER 10: FINAL ADVICE

Final Advice

You have now come to the end of the book for CSSE 11+ Maths Test: In-depth Revision & Sample Practice Questions for the 11+ Maths Essex Grammar School Test.

Now you are well prepared for the types of questions you will be asked in the exam.

- To recap, the maths test is comprised of **one** test, and **one** answer booklet is provided.

- There are a total of **sixty marks** available for the exam, and you are given **sixty minutes** to complete the test.

- You will **not** be able to use a calculator in the exam.

- When you are given your exam paper on the day of the test, make sure to read through all the information at the front and carefully fill in your details. You will be given time to do this before you begin the exam.

- The front of the exam paper will break down the basic instructions, so you can always refer back to this if you forget anything during the exam.

- Make sure you write your answers clearly in the answer booklets provided.

- Remember, when going through this revision guide, keep trying any questions you didn't quite understand, and check the answers to see if you are on the right track.

- Have a go at practising some of your answers under timed conditions, so that you are used to the feel of the timings on the exam day.

We wish you the best of luck in your Maths exam!

WANT MORE HELP WITH THE CSSE 11+ TEST?

CHECK OUT OUR OTHER REVISION GUIDE:

FOR MORE INFORMATION ON OUR REVISION GUIDES, PLEASE CHECK OUT THE FOLLOWING:

WWW.HOW2BECOME.COM

Get Access To

FREE

11+ Tests

www.MyEducationalTests.co.uk

Printed in Great Britain
by Amazon